The ABC of ANIMALS

Illustrated by Fiammetta Dogi

whitecap

A a
A is for Alligator

Alligators live in swamps and rivers in the southern United States and China. Alligators look scary, but if you frightened one it would probably just hiss and scurry away to hide.

B b

B is for Bison

Bison live in herds in America and Europe. American bison are also called buffaloes. They have shaggy dark brown coats in the winter.

C c

C is for Chinchilla

Chinchillas are small rodents with lovely soft fur. They live in the Andes Mountains in South America.

D d

D is for Dolphin

Dolphins have curved mouths and they look like they are smiling. They are intelligent, friendly, and playful.

E e

E is for Elephant

Elephants live in Africa and Asia. They enjoy eating. Elephants eat hundreds of pounds of grass and leaves each day!

F f

F is for Flamingo

Flamingos are tall wading birds. They scoop water into their big curved bills and strain out plants, shellfish, and frogs to eat. Fully grown flamingos have pink feathers.

G g

G is for Giraffe

Giraffes are the tallest
animals in the world.
Their long necks are
useful for reaching
leaves in the treetops.
They live in Africa.

H h

H is for Husky

Huskies are strong sled dogs from Siberia. They are intelligent and gentle and make good pets.

I i

I is for Ibis

Ibises are wading birds. They use their long bills to catch fish and mollusks in the water.

J j

J is for Jabiru

Jabirus are members of the stork family. They eat fish, insects, and other small creatures. They live in Mexico and South America.

K k

K is for Koala

Koalas live in Australia. They spend most of their lives in eucalyptus trees, nibbling on leaves and sleeping.

L l

L is for Lion

Lions live in Africa and India.
They stay in groups called prides.
Lions hunt and eat other animals.

M m

M is for Mammoth

Mammoths were an early kind of elephant. They became extinct about ten thousand years ago. This is a woolly Siberian mammoth.

N n

N is for Narwhal

Narwhals are small whales that live in the rivers and seas of the Arctic and in the Gulf of the St. Lawrence River. A male narwhal has a long tusk on the end of his nose.

O o

O is for Orangutan

Orangutans are apes that live in the jungles of Asia. They are very intelligent animals.

P p

P is for Panda

Giant pandas are very shy. They live high in the mountains of China. They eat bamboo shoots all day long.

Quetzals live in the rain forests of Mexico and Central America. Ancient peoples thought Quetzals were sacred.

Q q

Q is for Quetzal

R r

R is for Reindeer

Reindeer live in the far north of Canada, Europe, and Asia.

S s

S is for Snake

Snakes are reptiles. Many snakes make loud hissing noises to frighten their enemies.

33

T t

T is for Tiger

Tigers have thick gold and black striped fur. They live on grasslands and in forests in Asia. Tigers like to swim.

U u

U is for Urubu

The Urubu is a black vulture. It lives in South America and the southern United States.

V v

V is for Vampire bat

Vampire bats are blood-eaters. They make a small cut in their victims with their sharp teeth and drink the blood.

W w

W is for Wallaby

Wallabys live in Australia. They are from the same family as kangaroos.

X x

X is for Xenotarsosaurus

Xenotarsosaurus, pronounced "zen-oh-tar-soh-sore-us," was a dinosaur. It lived about 80 million years ago.

Y y

Y is for Yak

Yaks live in the mountains of China and Tibet. Their thick, shaggy coats protect them from the cold.

Z z

Z is for Zebra

Zebras are members of the horse family. They have striking black and white stripes. Zebras live on the grasslands of Africa.

My First Animal Alphabet

How many other animal names do you know? Fill in the spaces below each letter with new names.

A

Alligator

Aardvark

E

Elephant

I

Ibis

J

Jabiru

K

Koala

O

Orangutan

P

Panda

Q

Quetzal

U

Urubu

V

Vampire bat

W

Wallaby

B
Bison
. . . .

C
Chinchilla
. . . .

D
Dolphin
. . . .

F
Flamingo
. . . .

G
Giraffe
. . . .

H
Husky
. . . .

L
Lion
. . . .

M
Mammoth
. . . .

N
Narwhal
. . . .

R
Reindeer
. . . .

S
Snake
. . . .

T
Tiger
. . . .

X
Xenotarsosaurus
. . . .

Y
Yak
. . . .

Z
Zebra
. . . .

45

Index

46

Published in Canada in 2002 by Whitecap Books.
For more information, contact
Whitecap Books, 351 Lynn Avenue, North Vancouver, B.C., V7J 2C4.

Copyright © 2002 by McRae Books, Florence (Italy)

Publishers: Anne McRae, Marco Nardi
info@mcraebooks.com

Text & Design: Anne McRae, Laura Ottina
Illustrations: Fiammetta Dogi

Color separations: RAF (Florence, Italy)

ISBN 1-55285-421-3

Printed and bound in China by C&C Offset, Hong Kong